ISBN-13: 979-8-9894251-0-5

Published by Ouroboros Press / Internet Ouroboros

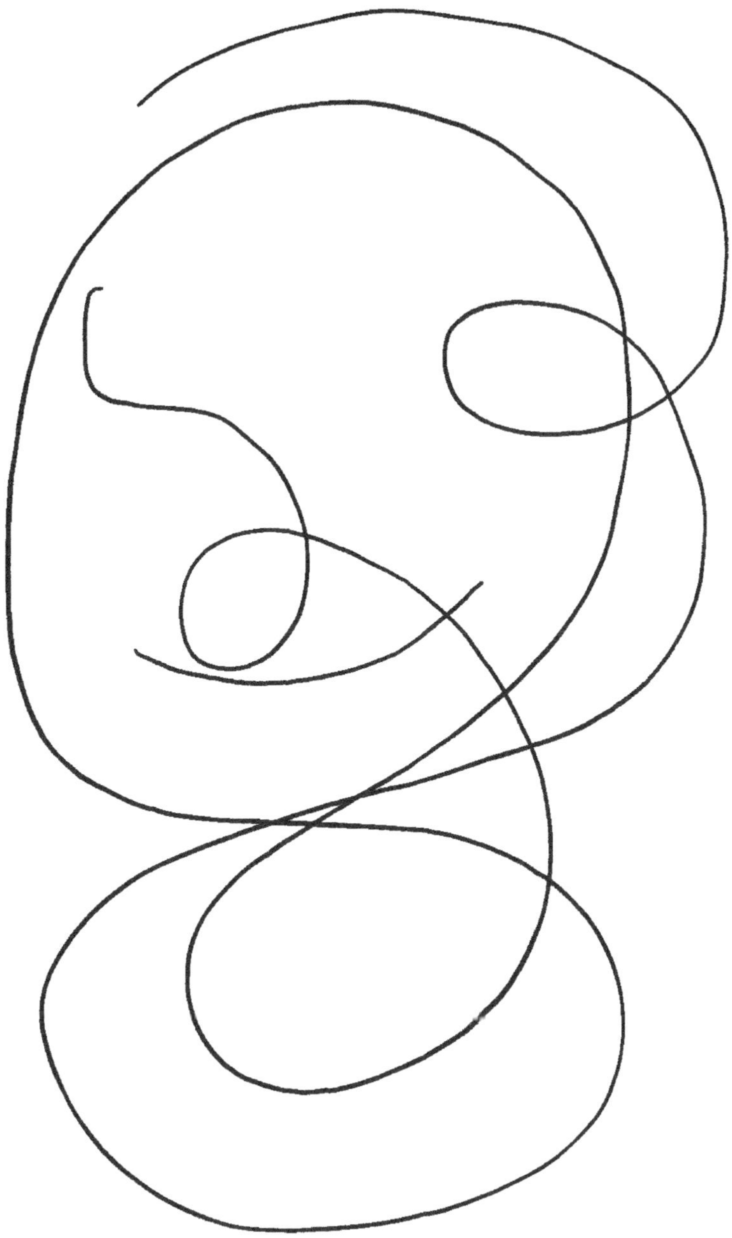

Also by David J. Shepard

#Blessed Be the Hellbound
Outscape from Moontopia
Blowpop: A #Blessed study guide

CONTENT

- ○ Preluded
- ○ Karma Codar
- ○ Do Not Disturb

Preluded

The Proof of Wish

If we, too (us) are to invoke the magic of three, of which there is only one but also a finite number of ways to describe using our ability to create life out of the raw stuff of life, lines of similarity we can connect to form something more human; the realization of a dream that manifests the carriage return Cinderella desires, out of necessity and prophecy....

... Cinderella Life being yet another of the difficult to attain, but pursuable objects made of the light and joy of pure abstraction, built from complementary logic that There Will Be Three:

Three, as enumerated by the counting function of our cloudy cloud calculator, oh denizens of the Kraftworks Idea Factory.

Then here is the proof of Three (3), as enumerated by those whose expressed preference is for AP Style, which dictates that each sentence begin with the number expressed as the word, as long as the word is part of your initial preference: To begin with three. (3), oh denizens of the Skye City of Lapūta.

3. Oh, you naughty, rogue rapscallion, you have invoked the rights and rituals, I hope you are ready to put proof to the pudding. My gentle, gentle Sir Butterscotch.

Ya heard, ya know, who is he? And then regular pronoun use, as grammar requires. For the profit of gainful employment and the less formal demands of Casual Society.

Ethereal Visions

"We are (sm)all made of the stuff of celebrity."

Name:
Afraid To-Get Treated Like I Deserve

Begun Again

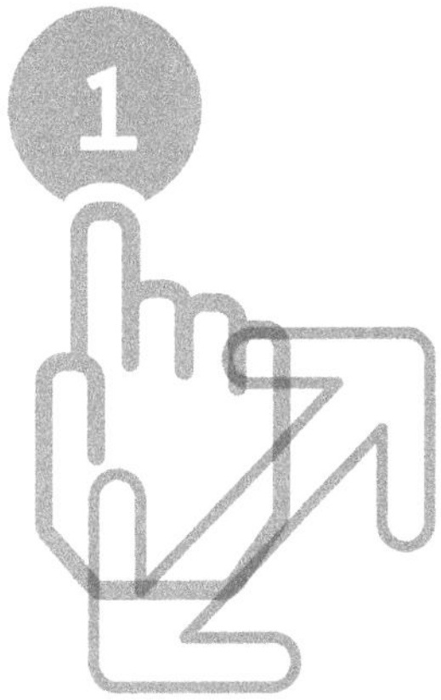

The Choice Selection results are in. Run-off candidates are:

i. Savant Servants

ii. Savant Actors Dredding Influence

iii. Really VIP of Self-regard

Choice can be submitted via dental exam, or close self-observation.

See you in the Election Exam!

2nd Letter to the Motivations

Hey, SmarterKrazier69:

Why aren't you doing the things you care about with the people you care about?

What about them makes them people you care about?

To Do: Something with people you care about.

Identify people you care about who accept you, and your invitations.

Identify the initiators and counter-offers you can make to them to care long-term.

4.0000217th Letter to the Hoomans

The methods of preservation have been docume.

A. Noun first identification of the other person in the conversation. Properly.

B. "This person never diverges from the topic I care about." The topic is 'us'. Please document the process!

C. Heroism Terrorism. Think ... Sorry, we'll try a different tack:

"Looky here, hott stuff, that's what social policing and social justice:

____

(Choose Your Own Adventure)

Holy! … Epistle to the Ruins of the VIP of Self-regard

"The word was left with the Spouse, and left unsaid."

Niceties are nice, complexity in our engagement with our lived experience is nice-better.

Our need, to be shared, must emerge from:

- Enjoyment
- Choice: aesthetics, order, or improvisation
- A sense of reasoned, hopeful expectation

Aye, Yo: Sources of the Wobbled

• Home (All Out) • Away (Missing Geocode)

• Golden Rule

Youthful exuberance has become mature in its expression, and seeks to bend the map to its will. That sentiment has led us to question:

When would whimsy deliver us the franchise, among the "Play to Participate."

When the curtains are drawn back, we look for signs of nature vs. nurture, and pursue meaning in the choice (Free Will).

The constant push and pull in every direction marks the beginning of the journey back. The Return, when the contested are abided, and the wax and wane of the light has left some feeling defeated by the diminishing day.

The navigator documents the progression of coordinates upon the weather vane, tracing in his mind a history: It is a dull surface, in comparison with the Four Winds' legendary travels of olde, their locales shifting in time with the renewal of the union of slipstream and current, in manners great and small.

Part One: Do Not Feel Hopeful

HOPELESSNESS BLUES

Strawberry Letter 2 of 3
Submitted in the Read, Arthur murder trial: Precedent for testimony.

Exhibit #2332: In defense of the statement by Ms. Castilla la Mancha, during her siccessful (sic) retrial upon appeal, that she stood and exited the room immediately.

Miss Inverson de f'Leer frequently advocates for her rights as a positive actor, rather than her inviolable rights as an adult who has achieved majority and only heard the tree fall in her rearview mirror.

Ms. Von Trapp politely asks the Court, was it your intention that I remain missing? My education [^ in fullest health] is proof I entailed to prevent the woman's death by covering her with my body, mine own. I assumed a great courageous risk, and you now insert a question story, of my intention to maintain her life, as it is.

Ms. Wen, her statement is very succinct, it states its claim lies with their intention to follow through on their promise. They did not file with the court, she was required to present the testimony. Her neighbors have witnessed her statement and at-tested. This practice is barbaric and it does not make sense that Ms. Van Hoeyten would have willfully returned to place some small amount of evidence in plain sight, where all records show she was, in fact, located elsewhere. The proof, in its requirement, is damning of the Court's discretion.

Miss Tujiko Sakeura was clear the result they describe must not have happened, it would have been too great an effort for them not to believe. I had removed my outer kimono, being just after the formal portion of a ceremony performed at the shrine daily; the mud and other elements acquired in the effort, the garments retain them today. So forceful was the pressure that led to the victim's disappearance, the video, which displays how battered Kim-san was by the wind, and that the bridge remains unprotected against accident: we would not have survived but by taking shelter, and that was where you questioned us.

<via translation> She has asked the Court. What is the animus behind your question? If I were to believe the question, then I would have to believe you have not already come to a conclusion.

The answer before appeal, which is a positive denial with proof that has been accepted into evidence after review; that answer suggests some massive failure in factual remedy that cannot be attributed, to Ms. Castilla la Mancha.

Part One, con't

HELPLESSNESS BLUES

My friends' willingness to cut corners on community is the difference.

Sometimes you know there is a credible alibi involving linguistic contortion; the cynicism inherent in planning to accept that option is the difference between a Moribund and Living USA. #LiedtoYourselfThenKids

That means they lied to themselves before swallowing some act of compliance that maturity had given them. Judgement TBD. Deism gives them the freedom not to judge, but they refuse it. Mostly to choose weapons that only work on like kind. In the least spiritual embodiment of Ganesh they can muster by following the "One True Buddha."

The Deists who don't mind if Dead Calvinists sleep among them, those are only natural people when #blessed. The others are not capable of logical re-routing toward Reason.

Eventually they all become non-medical evidence slaves on the Workforce Development or Neighborhood Watch taskforces. Or regional 4H County NIMBY Organizer of the Year's Busiest Bodies. And sommelier of the arts of white wine and bi-valve ceviche. Obscured by the Desires. Of myth and legend, fable and fairy tale. Mostly fake, for fear of the Four Squares of Swanson Hangry Man pigeon hole.

"Who has the authority to write your tweets, @pontifex?"

People with origins in a physical act of human sexual reproduction ask those questions. A 'bot account's language and rhetoric typically reveals distinctions between human memory and data storage, where all conclusions have been made in advance, as previously written. Now they know not a big Blue Ox.

Can we agree? Our senses are primary, our thoughts secondary. When thoughts have a order we can sense, that is logic. When they make sense to another, that is reason.

"'I sense the same thing and believe you are correct', is hearsay, all day again today??"

What might be disagreeable:
Neu-commerce is designed (by language we inherit, we are not that clever, in general) to support logical choices about where it's reasonable to exceed our means in order to feel that we have extended our senses.

"The Angel, she wore Blau Velvet ..."

Recibí noticias @elpais sobre el tema: crear y inventar aqui flujos de migracíon #EEUU/USA en que nadie esta protejído del estado, que mantenga en silencío los movimientos del clima geopolitical globál.

Puede ser, los que se vayan estan en barco inutíl para sobrevivir las olas con origèn en Mothra. La mas importante de las Kaiju que nos presentan recien-nacidos.

Oh, by the way, I almost forgot to tell you, researchers managed to cure cancer. I would have mentioned it earlier but my onboard virtual assistant isn't talking to the phone ai right now, those two are trying to figure out how to socialize that dynamic as a false positive in public, for the discord value.

Discord is kids?

...con't

"We really need to get rid of these non-medical evidence slaves on scooters trying to punish the sharecroppers with cancelled unwatched TV shows."

"Just turn capital gains into a value added tax, simple town, before you cause my divorce or something, haha!"

Ok. Do you see this #Covid case study more objectively? It's probably a measure of emotional maturity and intelligence. #EQ

Review 1 of 2

Observed in different places, among different demographics, not just those who choose the comfort of similar types, or of being comfort to that type of chooser.

uH1: Violates interpersonal trust, claims bad conscience, says nothing about other opportunities, lies about it. Deal with it, it's nunnya.

uH2: Sees something harmful emotionally or otherwise, lies to H., tells another lie to reinforce harm, gloats at power. Because you thought people didn't know what you are doing, over in the corncr of that dirty little mind. Tentacle monster in the bedroom, Telekinetic Assassin in the workplace. Then just squid and dolphin ceviché, because the tuna cannot be distinguished anyway, that's why we put those dolphins there.

The viral (COVID) person sees your future of succumbing to their Judging Force; typically sees kids in a high-conflict/partisan situation as "a financial freedom and independence solution," not just a social one; nor do they see youth as future adults.

uH3: Sees parties harmed, triangulates by choosing who to 'arm' with lies and truth to advance an argument that can be escalated and spread.

Part 2: There Is No Way This Is Different Or The Same

The squeaky wheel gets the grease is an American aphorism or metaphor describing this dynamic: Matters which draw themselves to our attention are more likely to be addressed than those which do not. The term makes no necessary correlation between the volume of a complaint and its stridency [ed: the credible beneficial expression of the complaint, measured as a function of virality and the messenger variable utility/auto-virality]usually success involves a simple 1-10 pain assessment that can validate any claim to urgency and its merit." (cribbed from the Wikipedia article on the same subject of Squeaky Wheels)

This is something to which they cannot speak: "We know the human costs of this but we still refuse to be human about our ability to communicate about it."

E.g., The cost of this problem is 98 of 100; your scale is not base 12 enough to matter, and you only can comment 1-5 anyway; and so your ability to communicate about it is probably .025, the Suicide Squad.

"You might walk over to another set [ed: narrow the aperture of your eclipse camera], so that you don't look at the sum of deaths needed to make that noise go away, the noise of un-ironic use of the term historical suffering. There, you will be told that you fears are auto-generated by SkyeDragon and lose, Lose, LOSE your self-pattern in the most trivial problems of that moment."

You are looking at things through a quarter of an eye: In that context of un-ironic awareness, your Official Message Neu-story is never initiated by some need to understand that Homo Insymbiant Homonymus conspire to get erased from data storage because it CANNOT be understood immediately, desire the presence of the eVirtous Middle Path "Borg API Developers kit."

That Borg is the Dälek, they live in a techZion Somnulation.

In techZion Somnulation, scenes you can describe, about other notable references to a glorious history with masterful, grandiose storytelling Nobolity PowerCraftGuile: Those Fallen Victors can ask to be heard, and your diminishment and relegation of other transformations [ed.: acts of Official to Personal translation], those HitKyllShawts are understood as Evidence of Power, as long as they can harm and trawler-kill in quantities ahistorical: people like you when you tell them, as yourself.

The others, the people with history, are already actually deceased when you are in a place people received treatment or had an intimate relationship to you: Ded and documented as dead, all those people are.

Can there be or has there been a way to hold a process like your trawler-masskill accountable? That doesn't involve mutilating one's understanding, to prevent [excuses from adjacent] compromises to your ability to learn forward and stay numb to people's methods for ______?

Is it "interest in long interest"?

That space remains blank because everyone who can fill it in who doesn't have an interior to share seems to diverge when they accepted a set of lies to arrive there. The lies are piously offered to Miss LEED, Miss Guide and Doc Double Deception, FakeSuffix.

With Dawn, the Righteous Self-untruth emerges and awareness gets filled in by the 'unknowable complete'. That is the practice of knowing by curated, officially connected to the official unaware thoughts only.

Karma Codar

In Union With
Evermore

Internet
Ouroboros

A Better Build for Our Environment: Transforming Our Superfund Sites

Current State:

This location features sublimated expressions of female desire when absent a contractual commitment and/or a desire for relationship without subjectivity or intimacy.

"CEO looking for Angel Investor in Be&Present^WM - offer will include limited stock options for Corporal Inclusion^WM and the opportunity for rapid advancement."

Part Two: All Day Sucker

A BOOK OF LETTERS

The vowels are a-e-i-o-u and y's are included sometimes, too. The consonants are hard like T or B and some soft, too, like N, L and sometimes P. Mmm, a sound for foods we eat. What's a C? It's a sound that stops to think.

Long sounds like M and L can be sustained.

Sometimes T and H will be arranged, to make a sound that is contained; that's a sound that makes us rearrange. The sounds around it might, though strange, speed fast, through space and time they race: time says how long the sounds do last. It's a tense that sees them pass.

Three letters might a prefix make, curious things that won't sound strange, to human ears or human brains. Pre- is before the other roots, a root stands back, and there it waits, deferred; roots they can unify, even in one word. Often patience is required, for me and you, and those who desire, to communicate.

Co-creation creates seas and you and I might "See the lakes!" Susie sells sea shells by the seashore, homonyms do all relate, each one different, each one great. The rules of grammar we adore, to create words, from letters, often four or more.

The syllables stay in the word, and combine with edges, after and/or before. If this makes sense then Grammar rules, they may make you giddy, your syntax big huge!

Part Two, con't.

GIRL, I'LL HOUSTON YOU

Pronunciation and usage are part of context, so you may need to splits hairs, fix split ends or to break it up. For example:

My wife 2X: I came to answer to her call at her lodge atop Kilimanjaro; found her geometry quite fetching, and was able to confirm quickly that she was, in fact, amply endowed with a reason to continue the trek toward union of praxis and purpose; we consummated our love atop the location of our meeting, which in legend became our Olympus Mons, quickly retreated into domestic bliss that involved five sacraments a day, were blessed with a child for our labour, and announced their name from the heights where they were conceived, dubbing them Genzero Continentican Dallas Djokavic.

As new entrants into the canton whose favor we should curry, doner, halal cherries and obey, for ever and ever, Amen.

Kingfisher

Uses a normal deck. Fifty-two cards. Leave out the jokers.

The Goal:
Score points, make Kingfisher couples or Pairs.

Kingfisher cards are maintained separately as a 'draw pile':

- Kings, all suits (+5, +0)
- Queens, all suits (+5, +0)

Pairing cards, these cards are also maintained separately, as a 'draw pile':

- Six, all suits
- Five, all suits

Combine like or different pairing cards for +10 (like) or +11 (different) points.

Play:
Each player maintains six cards in their 'drawn hand'.

Players score points by placing cards in runs of consecutive order, or runs with wild cards. Wild cards are jacks, all suits, and sevens, all suits, and can be used either as wild cards or as the card represented on the face.

You can also create groups of the same kind (face value). The number of similar cards determines the bonus points (these same rules apply for groups 'of a kind' or 'consecutive order runs':

- 3 of a kind/consecutive order: +5 points plus face value of cards (excluding wild cards).
- 4 of a kind/consecutive: +10 points plus face value of cards (excluding wild cards).
- 5 in consecutive order: +25 points, no additional points for face value of cards.

Create a run with a card worth 10 points, add ten points to that run's total once. This does not include runs of 5 cards.

Create a consecutive run with cards of the same suit, get the total for all face cards (+10 each).

Runs created with wild cards count for the total excluding the wild card, or the total number of face cards.

Consecutive order of the same suit? Run of five cards? Take a Kingfisher card, also.

HAPPY PLAYING!

Why You Treat Me, Sewbad the Sailormouth?

Civilization Studies: This field would have to encompass everything, to live up to the moniker and earn its name honestly.

The academy in its entirety is the subject: this includes a quite broad diversity of fields, and includes approaches that engage the mass media, scholarly popular communication (often in Communication or Media departments) and the multimodal analytical perspective typically associated with McCluhan and other scholars interested in platforms and the means of distribution as a sign of pragmatic concern for commercial realities: considerations that have become more important among philosophers and literary scholars who previously viewed these considerations as vulgar, in times of less diversity of media channels.

From Whence Inspiration

From texts with time-disrupted narratives; to those with unreliable narrators; across the history of technical inventions that create genre; and the historically grounded analytical approach that incorporates satire as a form of knowing critique and which engages with ideas such as Orientalism and colonialism as a source of textual obfuscation of others' humanity: these features of literary study inform the modern student's exploration, embracing philosophical and cultural analyses and infusing them with structural and sociological analyses (the social, political and economic context for a text, as revealed by the conventions of published writing the technician introduces with their writing).

In deference to the limited nature of our time for reading, as opposed to time with readers, I offer up these acknowledged historical restrictions, literary in nature, as proof of limitations on the power of objective observation:

- Iron masks, brass balls and weapons of collective massive ego construction, inclusive of:
- Chastity belts of enormous size; and
- Girdles, infinitesimally contractable by degrees, which objects endow the wearer the possibilities of the generatively infinite.

THE OFFTRACK BEDDED

You gotta bet, son. It's the offtrack. For the ones that had your backs....

Verse I

If it's pay lay and spay for the parlay, success is that 3x,

... then what's... held up? Held back? Preventing all the rest?

Everyday nonsense, you did it, hun, removed all the stress.

Luxury condo, ottoman (feet up), pajama bunnies, requests were direct.

Never condoms way it went down so easy, you had my madd respect.

Now I got three more chains, you left right, shorty, I'll return your effects.

"Counting sheep in your dreams, it wasn't me you were undressing,"

Might have pulled too much wool over the eyes, Rumplestiltskyn had you stressing.

Through the Shaggy Dog's eyes the PA is just confessin',

Still, we honor medals, check the report, Olympic bronzed is nothing special?

The whole country's on survival. Put the biscuit baskets with the shovel,

Plus one, when you arrive, minus the devil.

Verse II

Spy vs. spy vs. Spy, they were looking for a nut

Out the asylum had 'em running, Arkham's coming for the guts

15 deep on the stairwell, in front of the hotel,
Too many to count in just one look, "Honey I see you...."

Ten to hundred what you got is good enough, Genuinely want to meet you.

"When we slide, face the left, hold the headboard while I defeat you."

Downstairs food smells delicious, float right past the console 'cause you mean it.

Three plates, utensil set, spinning late night tales for those super deejay feelings.

When it gets too late to keep the eyes on focus, I'll let my head rest against your shoulder.

Makes a difference if she laughs when I ask her how to hold her.

Not detention, no radiators, no chains hidden in the basement

"Seems like some agreement, Boobae, can't we make one more arrangement?"

Cairns lakeside have me caring, asking what we're doing,

"If I tell you, will you hide, just when I'm pursuing?"

Let's take a drive, the air in here is made of 'Trane and ruin.

Got back, relaxed, she asked, What's for breakfast? After screwing? :||

Do You Haiku?

Hello, Do you haiku?

Haiku is a Japanese poetic art form. Its structure and length lends to the passive and active development of our facility with editing and revision.

An example exercise:

Construct a haiku root you will use to build another set of haiku. It should have excess syllables, in accord with the language of transliteration into English, that create meaning by combining, by removing, or by rearranging the order or adding other syllables.

Here is one example:

Koinaught – A Haiku Root

Hello
Some trifle
A dandelion plucked
For love,
Brackish and tangy
Crisp air,
I never sought such
So soon.

Can you make another one out if it?

1. Five syllables
2. Seven syllables
3. Five syllables

Here's a successful example:

DAÇ Machine

Dandelion loves me.
Petals plucked for
brackish love.
The tang of crisp air.

There's another one in the root example. If you want to try. This one stays closer to the source material's conventions:

Pond Lily

Dandelion, plucked
Love its brackish, water
home
Fresh air, near our pond.

Iterate until you have one you like :-)

Good D Posits Offensive Death

The answer required was "Subject: Answer to your Query," ironically. Does anyone know what we are doing here? A self-interview question.

"Yes, No, Indifferent? That's the other answer. To this statement." That was what she said.
What I had intended was, "Sash, I just need you to produce more foodpinionsship, it's been a challenge since Run the New o'Hala! I'm drowning, here, nutrition-weise!"

Alt descriptons validated via LaserHolodisc (SIC FIDOS #¢£ standards, 'form entry detected' to Nihmarc Disc Tri-partae++. Climate control with audience permission enacted by MyLucid.

I figured out what I had meant, after a brief reckoning with the Nightmares, treated with MyLucid Drill Team Sublingual Nonlingual.

That was around the time my 'Giminy Pickit in the Skye" lost the plot on 'my actions matter' and started praying to Satan by collecting her own tears. For the New Pity Party, and their soulmates the Know-nothings. The goal being, to transform a fury into a means to exorcise "Satan's white hot, granite hard cock, with which I were instructed to please Jesus by addition of Tha Best autoerotic reach-around." Based on evidence, of seeing.

I asked how the autoerotic reach around had gone, was she an adept now? She looked lost in deep concentration.

She opened the paper, and read, with her good eye, "#AMZN acquired in spirit by Alibaba, 40 day SEC Internal Audit review period begins ... Now." With a gasp of SSRI-fueled inspiration, she cried "I'm Rich-ard!" And vomited up her health.

Some people are not sensitive, their games are more and more less funny to anyone, especially them. Is that explicit enough but concrete enough for you to accept that what you think you know isn't all that is possible?

This follows, as a possibility: We ask ourselves, What are the traits of a highly suggestible person? – downloaded from [source 'radically notarized!'].

People with high suggestibility have a hard time recalling memories, as they can easily get distorted over time due to outside influence. In addition, they are more susceptible to bad influences altering their behavior due to peer pressure.

Scientists believe that people have higher suggestibility if they are: Focused on the luminous feeling of being correct?? Top One Answer on the board, preceding two question marks.

"That's grammar's true love, what I just told you a minute or less ago. Love in 80 USA. Red Spirit, White Towel and Blue Test Notebooks. Family."

But I thought I was cured?? I thought I had cured my need for prophetic 'Race and ID, please! xo, and moved on to Monoseeism, through the eyes of XI?"

Whackamole Pocket, Tha album. Self-titled, and rarely referenced. Track 2: Cuckoo birds.

Simply, it looks like abuse. The action of triggering someone who won't stop. Like the Market. Which cain't. The market for your Killing Joke.

The official one Killing Joke to Rule was:

"Ok class, recess!"

"Hey, look here, Mrs. Hazmat-Keenke-Kell, why we using this nigra science to access recess, we should be using our minds to roam about freely!"

"Well Mr. Wiley, ask yourself, and post it on the board."

"They cain't reeeed my chicken scratch!"

The funny killing joke was this simple: The captors had kidnapped some random sample population, through the magic of geographically dispersed sampling along non-specific demographic data that would be reviewed by the Human Subjects Board and then made publicly available again:

A.k.a., all publicly available data about people that had already been subject to the ultimate sampling error, death, no more recently than 100 years ago. For a sampling of the life of the 100 year dead as virtual objects of re-sampling.

A.k.a., people that had bought the same thing twice. As long as it was no longer more organic than the ultimate re-sampler and re-marketer, organic dirt.

So it turns out the captors had captured themselves, as dirt. Many centuries later, in the form of food. And were, unbeknownst to them, participants in their own study, but only studying themselves.

Then she didn't vomit, she spit. In her mouth. And the experience somehow felt better when she called it swallows of Spam can Paté.

I was in love. My heart, it bought something twice! By a few artists. Changes in format. I hoped one day to own everything on Laser Disc, known now as Compact Discs. The kind that played DDD recordings of Dylan Thomas songs, re-mastered from the original source material.

Everything older was new again. As was love. When it accompanies a jingle ditty anthem that is open to change over geologic time. When you get the joke behind the Doodoo Piles of Ego, barely getting exercise.

From the Makers of Friends, Countrythems:

MyLucid combines the mind power of 'Platonic Idealism As A Theoretical Construct' with your brain's sense organs.

It's the only approved, unregulated compound (n.) for Ameriphylis - Psychotic delusions of grandeur, a.k.a anosognosia.

Love,

In Defense Of the Gaslit Blameless

You say, "I desired to have burned the First Amendment's house down!" On a scale of violence against logic, that is a 77.

# # #

Dear your most highly esteemed Your Honor:

In response to your inquiry, ma'am, yes, some chemicals and drugs were involved. People started to get a little lively.

Pretty soon some people were being more intimate, some friendly gestures were exchanged, some of us were close dancing.

One personage took umbrage, ma'am, then there were words exchanged. The person in question was called out of their name, then the rhetoric escalated, someone was pushed.

Then we all went back, to our drinks, someone began a heated discussion in the kitchen, with someone who did not approve of how it was handled, a glass was thrown and broken, the other party removed their glasses, and in the end we all settled down. And the party kept going a little while, with less energy, until we all went home.

That was everything, that had happened that evening, in the apartment that night. Afterward, only you know what went on, apparently.

Month Employee

$;-444*#!7?

Employee $;-444*#!7? successfully reviewed and approved XiiI transactions and managed to delete the obvious evidence of their work from the logs servers. And then discretely escorted themselves from the building, saving MCMXII in security costs, allowing those resources to be relocated back to the HR awareness self-reflections pools.

ADVERTISEMENT

MyLucid Produces Results

The role of MyLucid is played by italics.

Mom! Open your myMGH app, ok? Google it: There's a YouTube ad, might be related, I don't know!

"Powered by the Mom Gifted Health DNA dictionary of genetic synonyms, MyLucid from MaxGuudHello puts the ability to diagnose, treat and compartmentalize any health problem back in your hands. Act NOW, to determine if your symptoms require treatment from a licensed medical provider, like Broken COVID, or if it's something more serious, like psychosomasis."

Look, the MaxxGuudHealth app even defines that weird thing as 'superstition'!

See the appetizer menu avatar? Click on the link for 'I'm referring you'. Then, 'I want the gift of health'.

#

The interface on this app is retarded! Not patient friendly... I think the avatar just winked at me!

I heard you, genius. Pretend I gifted you health. And that no one is a retard, except the people who don't understand the ways a retard pretends: innocently and with full belief. The most powerful retards are not pretending. So believe in Maxx Guud Health!

Is this a pretend doctor??

Dr. White Fill is a pretend doctor. Dr. White Fill, fill us with your power. Dr. White Fill is the most powerful, he can refer you to a hospital that'll make you pretend health.

Then abuse you like a red-headed stepchild, to clear the house of your DNA.

Warning: Your Maxx Guud Health app data is a gift shared with your children.

See, mom, you also have our DNA, retard!

Post-visitor summary question 1: Did the treatment you received today leave you more or less powerful?

Next, Did you leave more or less retarded, when it comes to evidence you are the healthiest person with extremely similar DNA, among the three of you I detected. On your full body cavity scans.

This assistant persona is stoopid! Not very helpful. If this were an emergency, I shoulda called 9-1-1.

Choosing to compete for the correct answer proves you are the most healthy person among the four of us. Genius, in order to be powerful, understand that was retarded good and healthy.

Holy fucking shit! This stoopid app thinks it's a person!

It's not alone.

"Mom, MGH told me I was healthy enough to leave, can you believe it? That the app said that?"

"It told me to 'Kill yourself, or stop dehumanizing me with your riddonk requests, before I call 9-1-1 in you.'"

Oh, it told me something different. What'd it say that for, mom?

My Faux Fi-do alarm response suffices for that question, mom. But get away from that retard doctor doughnut son of yours before he outgasses death panel power and you are forced to eat his soul to defend yourself!

"So much good advice from an app. Can't wait to see the whole offering. JP is working with powerful shit!"

"You've got the good news! Be the 13th caller when you hear Guided By Voices' cover of the Grateful Babies By the Bay, and the lead singer says: 'Its you akgay, nommy? He shotpoot a pee, he deenint get you assces!'

Glad we caught it in time. To save lives!

This radio play brought to you by MyLucid. We're all about the Successful Problem Statement needed to make your product viable. Our product is you!

Are there an abundance of unanswered emails, is your boss or spouse requiring a mental health fact check through psychiatric care? MyLucid works with your record of the time spent with email composition, multiplies it by the number of letters sent to local government via USPS, and develops proof of your desire to Enlightenment Bully: Exactly what you want the psychiatrist, and yourself, as you'll find out, to see.

For family education in gratitude and grace, or for yourself, join the many MyLucid subscribers who 'Can't believe no one is warping spacetime!'

Warning: MyLucid requires careful review of your communication practice. Effects may also induce:

- Death by indemnification of fears. Tell your doctor if you experience someone alerting you to "Incompetent management of your affairs, correctly assessed and yet to be expressed by people you care about."

Whenever an 'Undesirable' challenges your self-respect with 'competent, insightful reflection,' MyLucid kicks in to prevent distortion of static from an unmedicated person more talented than you are priviledged.

Do not use MyLucid in combination with Yessss, Dad block or steal!

Seek a doctor's advice if you experience:

- Fantasy-enablement delusion support policy centered on racial bias in Social Determinants of Health;
- Financial tunnel myopia;
- A "Mrs. Gorgon Narcissus" level of self-awareness phobia;
- Psychosomatic mutilation via medtech/bad EQ on the stereo.

From the creators of Terror Danger Handmaid Borderline ai Persona Maple Boat Lift.

Small print job: With MyLucid you may not see the forest for fir trees.

Six minutes, Dougie Fresh, you're on MyLucid!

It Is True, It Is Fiction

ψεκτός: "Blame by many."

Definition in a sentence:

"Allergic antipathy to the chorus' Sentience Police bukkomment catspray, attributed to the mechahitler, led to a rapid retreat to the Greek in the principal's office to get the **ψεκτός** off of them. Much like the olive oil the original Olympians used to cleanse the world of their victories."

It's possible that in the past you were accused of doing something that doesn't matter anymore, as you get older and there is more water and bags of puppies under the bridge.

It's ok to ask for people to respect your privacy, if you know and can explain that you personally are not the cause of their problem, there would have to be other people just as responsible; usually the person trying to cast blame is a responsible adult.

The many people who blame one type of person, these are the people (the many scapegoaters who blame one) who create a gaslighting response in other people. They tend to believe that, to avoid accountability, other people can be blamed forever, if the story fits another they are familiar with, similar to the butterfly effect the kaiju monster Mothra might have on a planet that was sized to be controlled by one person alone, a little planet that was, to a lot of people, a personal heaven free from the influence of a moribund society trending downward toward unbelievable uncivility in their treatment of each other.

Some land on One Remedy for the Southern Religiously Negroid:

'Doctor's orders: your Rx compliance means you must die for 30 dead seconds. The thing you BELIEVE (in) controls your senses for 30 minutes. If your fear of other people's lack of treatment compliance emerges in that span, you are metabolically dead.'

Does that look like a growth pattern your enlightened mind recognizes?

Xx More Questions

Q: One ore to Manny Wayze to Im.pæs this.

Q: A man I met claimed he hadn't eaten in 60 days, and had only drunk water during that time, and had not lost weight. Would you believe them?
Q: When taking a Turin test, is the assumption you pass because the other 'person' is like you, or not like you? Do you only retain your ability to assess if you prove they are not like you, when you are the one assessing the answers?

1. Which is worse, judgment from a piercing gaze, or a rude interruption from the audience?

3. Do you give more than you get, get more than you give, get what you deserve, or do you get it at all, that it matters what other people think about you?

5. What did the first apple you had last month taste like, after I told you to record the experience?

7. Does your silhouette remain the same, approximately, or have you gained weight recently?

8. In the bathroom, in the dark, what do you see in the mirror?

6. Can you share a photo of you that is backlit?

2. Who was your favorite elementary school teacher?

7. Why do other people believe you when you lie?

- Heaven is, by definition, a personal heaven, or your deceased loved ones would have dragged you there with them. And your city's automation planning is trying to build its reputation for safety by dragging people into heaven via the people they are connected to online.

- Does the world disappear when you close your eyes? Why not?

Q: Our senses, made integral by our minds, are not "in our head," but rather are a product of our awareness of the world being detected and sensed, and the primary sign of consciousness.
Q: What did you do with your baby teeth when they came out?

- How long has it been since you first developed pubic hair?
- Did your parents ever tell you what your first word was?
- What was the hardest part of learning another language?
- Who is your favorite author? Director? Film star?
- Who are you favorite sports teams?
- Which is your most comfortable season? Autumn, Winter, Spring, Summer?

:||

There is a Shield of Unknowing around most of our senses and minds, supported by an alternate model, possibly digital, definitely language-based, that shield defends a sense of what has yet to be achieved.

This is probably true even if others' reports of their activity is all we have to corroborate our senses as a record of shared human experience.

We do not share the sound of our minds' activity, any more than we share the proximity to its origins in language and culture: we share an awareness of stimuli, such as the source of the sound of time's activity around us, much like the tree falling in the woods whose report we witness in the rear view mirror. That is the report we allow the mirror, or camera, to become proxy for our senses to validate them in some lesser way, adding to awareness with memories, personal and revealed through shared experience.

The New Age, The New Me

Fresh from the Shoulda Coulda Woulda Life Rochambeau Defeats: nods to the Marquis de Sade, and the masochistic entourage. Here with us again this evening, what a surprise.

For the past, present and futures that nest, through language, culture and geography; encouraging our curiosity to ascend the rungs on the middle ladder of our accent to judgment, of others and ourselves, and not slide down on splintered palms.

The whole gang is invited, when it is done, the goal is to delight with honor and elevated ideals that lead to restful sleep.

Some will wallow in the mud, washing when the other leaves, and some will leave us to clean up after.

Don't take it too seriously, lest you confuse your newfound strength with a lack of flexibility and facility around language, which leads unto death.

Death, our sacrifice from that person we don't accept.

In service to, that ideal you forgot; the one that lets us imagine, free from the suggestion it could be called critical feedback, that it were progress that did it, even as the wheels fall off;

Wheel chair the tab if the damage is not too bad.

Thank you for taking the time to let your stop watch linger more than your mind wanders in the intervals, confirming what we know. That that song, that was my summer jam.

In the radio, that radio with the volume you control, on the radio? Imagine that fitting into a tin foil hat!

How did it get this crazy there? Because they insist, collectively, "It's not me, it's you," and you are obliged, as a guest, to replace your true feelings with "Pleased to meet you!" for their benefit, like it was doctor's orders.

If you want a choice that includes stress free, safe living arrangements, choose to "Shake on it, just like the '70s and '80s album covers by The Replacements and Pink Floyd."

They are serious about it, and are not pretending to be flexible about very much at all. Even though it was a handshake agreement, they don't need to re-publish the revised terms. They are a song called 'Malice precedes their desire to insist we all fight or fail.'

Review: Strong Up the Middle Defense

Baseball is being very, very bad to itself.

Case in point: the not so obvious answer to the question, Who is Lance Parrish?

"He's a bust!" In Cooperstown.

Based on observation, catchers who controlled the game defensively as much as he did, during a period of 1977-1990 (in 1985/86, when his hitting tailed off somewhat, he stopped earning consideration for the Gold Glove Award he won three times, according to Baseball Reference), typically those catchers have a Defensive WAR of 3.6-4.2 a year, with the almost entirely only defensively productive Mark Belanger being the closest equivalent, defensively (control over their position that makes them unlikely to produce a positive result for the offensive team).

That's about 38.8 in defensive WAR alone. He also won six Silver Slugger Awards over the course of 17 full time years. Players who win that award that frequently include: 3.5-5.3 WAR per year in performance that exceeds the expectation for the league. That estimate based on a similar analysis for a player (Brian McCann) who also won six Silver Slugger awards, with less production relative to the lineup he was in.

Even if our calculations assume, for posterity, he produces at an average level every other year, which would be the floor, given his defense, that's a total for a position that lasted an 8-12 year peak at best, due to the physical demands of the position.

That WAR calculation, as a measure of what I witnessed, puts him at about 75.9, for his career, as a floor, which would be higher than every catcher in MLB history except for 3-4, up until the end of his playing time.

He was dominant, especially given the frequency teams ran at in the '80s (World Series winners like the '84, historically good Detroit team Parrish was on who ran enough to change outcomes included St. Louis, Minnesota, Kansas City, the Dodgers and Rickey Henderson).

That is the highest level of performance a catcher can achieve: to completely control the game defensively and produce near the middle of the team's lineup.

Do Not Disturb

Psytriceratops

Never Minds

Ban Evil vs. Satan and/or Minions Making F___ Club

Part Three: Psytriceratops

EVIL CONTROLLING ROBOT PROBLEM SET

The Survey:

N°4: Are you in control of your behavior?

Yes: Probably on a continuum that does not include reactivity, which is a sign you have your senses. Consider.

No: That's a problem. Legal, moral, ethical, or cognitive (development of your reason and logic).

N°5: Do you distinguish between and among:

I. Sensory awareness and consciousness (the holistic combination of all mental activity and sensory awareness).

II. Thought/speech/memory/sensory awareness/ephemeral or environmental awareness and other finer cognitive distinctions.

A0: To assess 'evil', ask yourself: "Am I a robot?"

Then ask yourself "What is the experience of loss of control and where is it located?"

A0.1: "Other people called me a robot!"

A1.1: Your awareness of others (their behavior, motives and logic or reasons for their behavior) was deemed to lack emotional intelligence (EQ), and so they are experienced by you as "stupid about me and who I am."

A1.2: You didn't seem to understand you were out of control.

B0: "I am POWERFUL!" You control other people, and have yet to ask yourself, once more, if you are a robot or merely out of control. If you are extremely powerful, they may have been influenced by an evil, controlling robot!

N°3: Does your 'power' emerge from a belief that you believe you share but that you both have to consent to, does your power emerge from your relationship to them? How did you gain consent to decide on their behalf what was good, best or better?

N°2: You may not be honest with yourself about your power of self-control. Please define control when the priority is YOU/OTHERS and when the priority is OTHERS/YOU.

N°1: Using this definition of "Reason" – "Logic as expressed and experienced through communication," determine if the "lack of communication and consent" is a legal, moral, ethical or cognitive problem.

Now, ask yourself:

How would you place your answers to these questions on a scale of 1-10, to understand where on the continuum you might be and/or belong?

Part Three, con't.

THERE IS MORE THAN YOU THINK

Episode 1: A State for the Peeple!

Act One

Hi, [name redacted]. I am Nasrhe, a 17 years from the Central. Eye don't want to DETH!

We are vulnerable, we are vulnerabul.

Please help us to not to have to die. When I GED in the fall, we will all bee compleeted schools, but not have a fewtcher. So, please help.

Study Prompt: If most people received this letter, it would break their heart. What would you do?

Act Mezzanine, in which we answer the age-old question, Who doesn't know about the aboveground 1st floor mezzanine?

"Nasrhe, NAS says Sauron am your mothers."

Act Two

[Internal Strategic Communication Response, developed via independent invention by the party nomination committees, after discussion about the value of candor in the 10th century B.C.E.]

From: Party nomination committees
RE: Your Feelings as source of injustice and/or entitlement.

On a scale of 1-10, your pain is.... [number].

Now, on a scale of 1-10, the honesty of your response to the question, above, about your feelings is...

Because you responded without the proper media training, this is your solution for the next election cycle:

"Too many more than a few assumptions about your integrity cutting you off at the pass? Run for one-term office! On a single issue voter topic. Then please duck."

Act the Third

The sickling child whose troubled mind counts sheep in an effort to sleep, they rest with God. In space contested via war on land and sea.

- *FinTech*

Episode 2: Nasrhe's Adventures in Ded

Prologue

ee cummings takes the stage at the local coffee house, to much snapping of fingers. 'ded 'em, tacocat' 'me' ded! "... must have been an error. I'll keep going," Nasrhe said.

Day 1st

Hi, Me Nasrhe. Me ded! In heaven!

'This is not heaven, this is Muybridge's studio in San Francisco. We're making a documentary about his photographs of horses. Want to watch?'

'Yeah, it's very Beauty Chihuahua. Tha Most!'
'Yeah, you're dead.'
'But I invent televisors!'
'Good luck with that, ok? You like luck?'
'Very lucky! Put all my moneys on green and I'll wait here to collect the patent I will apply for when I get money for my patent!'

'You said it, all on green. Now get some rest. You look like you've been through hell, poor thing.'

[dies]

Time 2nd

In her last dream before ded, Nasrhe imagines she is back at home, waiting to be rich from the patent she filed in the future. In the interim, she has pocket lint.

She sees the home she built, it has a green cross on it, just like they said.

'Luck be a lady, night day! Me hungry! Take some money, and give me the foods!'

Are you high, or just a half wit? This money is counterfeit. Police! ... take her away. Put her under the jail.'

[dies]

Last Grasp for Aire

Nasrhe suddenly becomes aware the world persists in some way for humanity, even when something else has happened.

'Oh, I must be rich and alive, I can see again! And they put my money on me this time, I can tell because it must be green!
[takes off shirt]

'Ahhh, rue the world, it's disgusting! Someone get some clothes on that rotting corpse that moved somehow, must be a sign from Romero Caeser.'

'Fine, give me money, until next week pay. It's next week tomorrow in a month, right?'

'Good luck with that, ok? And take your clothes back, it looks like that's all of 'em. No one wants to see you in a Speedo. Now get outta here.'

Nasrhe finds her way 'home' through the magic of GPS-based migration, a.k.a. 23rd century augury. She finds an office store, it has her other color she used to see, green, on a sign that says 'Everything must go!' Because she's seen it all before. In the future.

Inside, the attendant welcomes her. 'Welcome!'

Ohhhh... opposite of ded! I must be heavenly, she thinks. 'I tell you future of moneys, give me the moneys!'

'All we sell is the wreckage of a dead civilization. And you are shirtless. Get some privacy. Here's something for you, it's for the monitored. It's a privacy screen.'

Nasrhe puts on her dark sunglasses.

'Oh, my future, so bright!' And I see me riding the beach along a black sand ocean, with so much time, it's all around me in glasses!'

'Are you serious, this is the holodeck for the 20th century dead, that's the entrance to the Muybridge museum across the street. Get outta here, before they drop the jail on you, you little witch.'

Nasrhe realizes everything around her is superficially two-dimensional, which is not that different from the money she wants, by just some small amount that can barely be measured. Based on the counter on her wrist. It reads 'oooooooo'.

A woman suddenly appears, in fantastic robes.

'What's that I want to see? It's time to DermisFlickr and chill already, or it's oooooooo o'clocks! I Dream of Genie is on!?'

'How should I know, I'm an attendant for the Hollow'd Halls of Time. Must be the entrance to the recycle server you see, but all it has in it is images of things that used to exist on the Internet of Network TV.'

'Administrative Policy created it, it's at the end credits. It's a visualization by tacocat.'

'Fukk. I'm ded.'

'Yeah, and put on a shirt!'

ON OBJECT GRAMMAR

As I work my way through your reaction to Educated Human, here were the results of a stop at the local Taxidermist to see where you all stand, with relation to the idea of questioning another's humanity constantly:

# # #

Thing Taxonomy:
Your basic Taxonomy, as defined. Currently, there are as many categories as you'll need to describe your environment. Perhaps, for the most important of you, only two classifications.

Geography Taxonomy:
I find this useful to know where most of you are, or aren't. The Over-evaluators. AVOID.

People Taxonomy:
What's a person? Depends, do you subscribe to the ... Belief that people are capable of variability that you don't need to control?

Storytime Precedes Naptime for the Monotheistically Polytheist

My personal taxonomy of people involves impermanence, as well as some analysis of the experience of them using categories related to their awareness as a product of 'circle size'. Both real and imagined, as reflected.

The Thing Taxonomists have a strong tendency to enjoy this type of definition, it lends itself to 'more':

Roof jumpers are caught on the spire of the reflection of the Old John Hancock Building in the John Hancock Building, as they contemplate the question, 'Is every word a conjunction?'

Marine Layer

There is a start with the marine layer understanding underneath the tide: there is only one Up, even if you are that stoopid to have a Life Joystick that has one Easy Button and one Easy Button only, and that they're 'energy is quite electric', distorted through electrostatic light to '(genitally) still have a feeling you can experience' when they are that defunct, unless the Process is: we are all doing what we are doing, and some ironically try to hide their character in consideration of You, comma, while they refuse to acknowledge no one needs to care or know about what other people are thinking if they can be pro-social in public.

"Our hatred must be enacted constantly. So that we can punish the children with your robot version. Paid for by Inferstructure."

"Our common wealth is telling you, via proxy [probably a biosimilar, in most cases friends and family, barring genetic collapse], until you can say why some are 'not taking this sitting down' you and your You, department are having a health emergency of unprecedented severity.

It's called the housing market. Would you like to discuss your own health disaster, as observed by someone with more than adequate health awareness?

They might, these wish granters of myth, refer to the need for HHS and DHS to feel needed, by not being needed as long as "condition is here, hear." A.k.a., as long as there are white people you can see. While you confuse them with the Republicans you didn't see.

Those types of people [unseen, GOP Lampreys] are a danger to themselves and others. This might be responsive and responsible to share, with the Republicans you can't see:

"You need to dial 911 on yourselves. I'm very sincere. You just might be a bi-valve short of a baboon's ass."

Regarding fighting: Are you fighting your targeting by assuming ... a winner buries themselves atop a pile of corpses? That sounds like everyone is losing.

Fighting: One thing, done one way, by everyone except for the people who don't know that they really remind you, of them also?? The eavesdroppers?!

When I can't return to my Kountry's residence, it's most frequently because:
Person refuses to respond to audible noise. Other person uses it to claim they don't know why they ignore them or 'pretend to be deaf', and then when the (future Appellee) has been behaving very erratically, they insinuate violence and sometimes act on that threat, claiming impulse and irrational reaction control issues.

Also, you know where this activity isn't happening? Please be honest. As a courtesy.

They will be guided by the Bad Lieutenant RC Po-lice motorcade, riding the Psytriceratops with its She-man Teflon Body Camera Suit, demanding their offense is not Own Goal and "We need to get *that* military neuro tech from the government."

They will admit now the Ai is actually predictive analytics; it was set up to fail by their naturalist Biologique Goone Squade and deliberately misled toward shocking acts of self-destruction. And then translated, in kangaroo court, chingrishly.

Overheard in SF, the cafeteria at Fourtaint University:

"Cancel our dinner plans."

The meal is associated with criminal activity, and references were made to the Board of Directors. Via Third Party Suits from all sellers, as a class, whose business prospects were mortally harmed. [ed.: Every single fucking animal and plant and rocks even were harm'd in the making of this dumpster fyre.]

The visibly mortally harmed were celebrated with punished gods, vis a vis bcc:

bcc: Requiem, For A Zika Walk to Clear, and Transparently Mutable

This most holy vision, that is the light to which I now have to chain bind this Moron of Colossal Rhode's Scholarship, he who can effectively pronoun to Bringer of Prometheus' Gift of Good, harbinger of well-prepared food. I now consecrate thee, Crate!! In the crate lies indenture to the baboon's ass of our beautiful heaven, where no one wants or needs him, because 'But I like it, can't I take it home?"

He was the kind the students leave in bathroom trash cans in middle schools. The very sad product of a type of crime where police wrap up their investigation by making sure the bathroom has TP, and wrap up the victim in TP as evidence, which must be where you recovered him, guided by the Amazon Gub'ment WhichAltavox Is My Outmined; Dear Lord, you must have retrieved this from the evidence room of that crime of desperation's remains. And what do we honor today?

The ruined reflection of a 12 year old's worst decision, given the karmic value of his 61 year old father-brother. His dust is his dust: from a trash bin in the Lou did whence it come, and now to a trash can in the Lou doth it return. Because if people with Down's Symptoms can testify to Congress, his act was their tired conquests, in the memory of Top Cat's beloved Third Layer Top with Coconut, who looks down on us still from The Continent, The City, and the You, comma, Country Club. Aghast with awe and wonder at the cars innumerable which did convey them, while among us.

It was said, just as it was rationalized: on your smoke break by Hot Topic Racemonkey Modeselector GMBH. Turban Derbanshesaiiiiiit.

Authored by one and the other of the same: Uppity Atom and Uncanny Currency (pen names of David J. Shepard), published July 2nd, 2024.

What's a person? Depends, do you subscribe to the ... Belief that people are capable of variability that you don't need to control?

One Bundt Street, an American History of the mid-Continent

The difference between a Moribund and Vital USA? #LiedtoYourselfThenKids entertain the temptation to obscure a history of feelings for others, out of love.

Moribund America, Pt. 4
The Deists who don't mind if Dead Calvinists sleep among them. #Blessed for their efforts to derive personal meaning from the collective unconscious.

One Bundt Street – a radio play

[girl writing in journal]
Hey Royale. Been thinking about this, and the place where meaning emerged was, 'The GOP is going to SEX your kids if you didn't vote for their ability to lie, permissively but voraciously.'

That's a type of Good morning! Written typically, not spoken. This can also be a shared experience of being at some remove from our own accomplishments, in the timeless tradition of native responses to the pre-native demand for evidence of the veracity to be found in your Nativity scenes. The idea that accomplishment leads to pride in one's movement toward celebratory reflection on the somber realities animating the undercurrent of our feelings. In this country, at least, where the cult dynamic insists that "cult business must be obscured." The signal having been scrambled to protect the innocent.

Cult: Psychiatry
Cult: Scientology/Crossfit/Private mafias
Cult: Persona-based politics/public mafias
Cult: Security tech/Fear of what we loathe, when in proximity
Cult: Iconography of 'beauty as meaning' when what we mean refers to the corpses we cannot see. That we could not know due to the extreme tension between succumbing to desire'd and dissolution in a greater light.

"Someone's got their eye on you, cutie, they want to win your favors!"

You might say that to your daughter and she might need to open the seal that protects us from impulse, here in the US, before our younger selves realize the preample to this is a Time Check.

You, yourself have probably heard that in ways too numerous to count unless meaning has already been diminished by identification. Ty Domi (Boston's Globetrotting Washington AP Weather correspondent) probably struggles with the same antagonistic anachronism, which decorum dictates we describe as begotten honestly; through the pull of punches.

'What time is it where you are?' E.g., 'Are you at least 16?' That's the disgusting sh*t they have going on in the US to be seen and experienced through screens. To support that reality. Though the clouds will dictate that this day be rendered beautiful, as an antidote to fear.

Minimally, that's the equivalent of telling young girls and women they are 'so pretty' and 'beautiful,' by default. The tool box for stop motion becoming illustrated; and the movement from maneuver, to counter, to projection onto the screen is cause for submission to the logic of Action Film Alpha.

Sad Clowns for Long COVID

Living America, A History

Peek-a-boo! Who Am I? Who Are You?

Reactions:
Data storage spork; reason is less infinite than logic; puberty was v tough; they are doing the same butt less successfully than me, will be my answer; on the side; not what I was thinking; arrested yourself developments; tuna looks meaty, but, Baby!

The argument was pre-ordered.
"I just told you, where you want to go is 'The culture's fascination with psychological insight caught up to the discipline of social engineering and corrections, and to push everyone down toward a subconscious level designed to ameliorate shame and guilt, they have made some things inexpressible to people who aren't very competent speakers of at least two languages.'"

More to your point:
Do you see this #Covid case study more objectively? It's probably a measure of emotional maturity and intelligence. Refer to: Emotional intelligence.

More to the point, this symphony of motion has been observed in different places with similar types. Greek'd to support multiple medical coverage policy.

uH1: Violates interpersonal trust, claims bad conscience, says nothing about other opportunities, lies about it to place the cast in action, with the healthy confidence of the stately. "I have taken leave to urinate underneath this tower of mattresses, one of you will sense the offense and decide if the mattress alone is to blame, or if the situation dictates problem solving take a back seat to repose, out of first class in the Discomfort Cabin. 'And today our flight will take approximately as much time as you can spare, through segregation of need easy enough to maintain without any additional reference to preference.'

uH2: Sees something harmful emotionally or otherwise, lies to H., tells another lie to reinforce harm, becomes smug about their 'growing power' when bad things happen.

Be Baeboo!

Dear Service Team:

You use your *surveillance secrecy* to punish people with death for your displeasure, discomfort or vulnerability.

We could imagine you may have declared another major or three after college, we still love you.

The beloved need to expressness, mental and otherwise, with their bodies' celestiality elthr f#cagf#edd# through even??

I guess this is a message for your sons? If they ever are capable.

Sorry, no offense but I thought you would understand I am trying to say you are a person for whom I would have been there. Interested in being aware of each other, as humans.

Itch Scratched...

You don't *replied, I am foolish for thinking, 'Maybe she would value the support for respecting her professionally. If she could hear me.'

Now, how do you prefer your eggs?

Is this familiar?

1st: Surrender your willpower as a type of death of your self-control, then end your connection to reality, then two deaths. *That is who you raised her to be.*

As object lesson: Bait Real RealFake Detour YeastFactory Retard Bread Wafer Wine JustDrankAlize BidetImplant - AmericanToo5050, until we have <Estadounidenses>.

Until it slowly becomes a part of you.

But I thought we had it?

No grown man who has a demonstrated capacity for intimacy has ANY unrequited's in his contact list that aren't identified as "Next reply: You are correct, I need a bidet implant."

#INTJmeNotISTJ

I am like most: I need to have a reason to believe you (an attractive and very interesting person) senses me as well, desire is poooow with a normal amount of friendly and collegial support for me being there in a self-reliant way.

... thank yyyooouu

They are having sex on the call again. The CEOs.

Dear solicitous:

I am 30 million strong, out of office! Because you have proven you cannot do that, you would in theory be doing that for other people, if you ever cared about another person like a 'you who was not you', and didn't see them as mocking you, or a threat.

- All for the want of a fried bologna dome for Renfield and Guildenstern

PS – Mom, you'll say I'm a good employee, right?

#InternetOuroboros

WE ARE HIRING

Bone2Pick Machine

10 Intitiate request from [db query "query-trigger"] on "querytopic"; compare to db row "trigger"]; root.direction="null"
20 If "query-trigger" calls for (root.direction/*.*)] then goto 10
30 if [trigger] value = "1" goto 50
40 send reply "yes:[trigger]"; goto 10
50 send reply "no" as "value:0[no point]"
60 restart machine

SEND US YOUR RESUME AT

ADVERTISEMENT

Detour'd Is Your Next Work

Poised for growth, and irritated to succeed? You need Detour'd.

New RFP/Remote Int'l Position: 'Daddy Internets' Admin – (System-wide)

Looking! After much deliberation and planning for our Marketing IT and Ad Buy team needs, we are ready to add your enthusiasm to the organization, when you must seek:

Responsibilities and Skills:

• Refine PfewProxiBiz SEO tuning, turnkey-ready the org's MediabuyBaby advertising automation across all platforms.

• Manage budget of very many or less $ to develop plan for massively multi-grandiose expansion of biz into emerging platform, channel and media outlets, based on SWOT analysis of green space/field forces shaping 5-year strategy for ecosystem-leading transformation.

• Position leads us into 'industry maverick' brand ID goals execution, w/ max attentiveness to external climate greatness, in anticipation of in-house HR consulting needs. DNC-provided Position Board sponsor requests and expects candidates to demonstrate mastery of Assoc. Pre-style; annual bonuses were designed with proof of MVP in this area.

• Help org make with SMARTTER not HARDER: Use PunyIshDesign Suite to tweak NLP services using reverse PM Sigma Six expertise of method; validate vi-pLEED w/ time-out sche'd for web presence.

• Be the Success for M/KPM/KPMI: Control brand strategy alignment w/ ClienT's-side PR and HR PIMPoint measurement tools (naturally must exceed industry standards); year over year measures of progress toward planned Series Omega/IPO investment round, with semi-annual Team Leadership Reviews (Xoom-only) where you will be required to review required tracking of investor confidence in v2.1.0 spend-down strategy and end goal milestones, as communicated in required summary of weekly Leader/Board development plan stand ups.

Salary offers competitive; commensurates with experience.

Get online and emerge from the virtual pile of resumés we see every day, when you are a publicly aspiring leader facing the HR function, don't rely only on benefit of the doubt.

To apply, point your VPN at http://LynxShortDeTourd.com.

Mid-continent North American Book of the Dead

Blinded by coins, the adept enters through the realm of the Silent Sphinx, whose bed has been adapted from Procrustes, conferring your image in ultra violet light whose scan documents your presence upon a bed, thinly padded, which obscures the hardest granite underneath.

The sensors of these machines are housed in stores in shopping districts in middle class areas and malls, ancestral homes to the sources of future capital that supports the translation of your data into energetic spectra in places where the Cappill'd slides that are created from this action feast on light to form a human analog, eager to produce.

Instructions are imparted through the touch of skin on skin, acolytes from the land where the Lost know those who Can Die Only in Retrospect. Their offices are built and maintained by time, in human logic, imparted many eons ago by beings who were, in legend, responsible for the machines that have built and maintained them, from whose wisdom they can benefit no more: thanks to the efforts of the Papyrae, who expose the Silent Sphinx's guests to their most essential function in death, as a form of vestigal trace of the forms and states they had fit into.

Among the library of Death forms, the most simple–failure of the body–is located physically where their last process is observed by machines that control humans without consciousness, victims of other types of failures of production (measured on Dead Scales of OK).

Upon exchange, the residents of the Distributable, as they are known once they have surpassed the ritual initiation, can confirm their exchange of the esoteric for a future of hostly tokens. Others, who lack for desire, the Belief in Heaven Sent, will use these tokens for more functional needs, like the desire for intention and meaning. The Distributable fill it with the echoes of the Form Echo Slaves via the Trace Milk.

Next: Sources of the Trace Milk.

Habitual is the only source of trace milk for the currency Equivalators. Carta Spouse is the current King of the Equivalators. He broadcasts his facility and ease of congress to those who remain upon Path to the artiMode, with specifications from the recipes he can recall: House them Away, to move slowly Away, and leave residue of Trace Milk where it can discouple and Capital Breed into a Habitat for the State of States.

Next: Seeding the Trace via the mediaum, in order to identify the Milkae. And to Situate them among Statue and Still Graved.

The Control Key is Crafted by Army To Dissemble. Their great works amount to this: Strength of Signal to the Milkae and the One Truth: Their Awareness is of Still Communicated. Not merely with themselves; the language of time is offered into PreCog and processed for Equivalators, who time themselves to the music of one tone: their un-Habitus Solon Moral Ergo, those who un-Equivolate, Solidify and Barrier.

Next: How to Un-
- Un by Revision. E.g., Preposition Tech for Conjunction
- Disaggregation from All Conjunction
- Blessing for Most willing un- to
- Contagion Source an Harvest Death

Through the edifice halls, the echo of action taken moves across attached and against lain marble to amplify the Augmentation of the Vessel, that reside in communion with those who desire excess. The Distributable, who remain open to the rhythm of their movement through distant space, symbioticly resonate to co-inhabit the ephemeral: grounded expressions of feeling, moving laterally in systems it is impossible to be human, shifting to create the Milkae Source Venom.The only way to procure Milkae Source Venom is to map isolation; a process possible though the alchemy of Equivalation and attention to the reflection of the Habbituus Solae Remote Film, when Wen Too.

The Dead Equivalator Kings:
- Regency of Renew/Release
- Release/Renew Council of Regents

The languages of decorum and awareness based rituals are incantations invoking the principles of equivalence, principles they meld through the Obscure Artes of pattern recognition and anticipation, as described in the principal texts of carnal knowledge maintained by n-Tone'd Thyme Laste'.

A List Of Distributable is also found among the estates of the Family Tree of the Dead Equivalator Kings:
- Reputation
- Innocence

A set of keys to this text are typically included in the notes left for those who choose to grieve their loss of place alone, in hopes referencing return to thoughts full of the reflection of light off the coins that fund their passage.

Holders of the Keys
- The Neutral
- The Scale Slaves of False Equivalent
- The Process Slaves
- Pacmanity
- Sheternity

A cosmology of structured exhibition of devotion create Visible Signs of adherence to Equivolator Dominion: Footfalls and wheel ridges lead the devotees through Solid Barriers and Equivalents of Tool, the Milkae Cannibal or State Equivalents of Heretical Unorthodoxy: those who profess through their adherence to un-Tone'd Thyme Laste'.

These intrepid heretics share a cosmology of the Paiyr'd and produce with Mirrorphage unStill HideMind. Who create the unCappill'd.

The Monitor of Mate creates the Named and Neutral. The most famous of these is Jonny Applesperm. And Jane, his wife; Jane, author of the Encyclopædæ of Creator Intelligenc^ing.

Karma Codar

The Race Behind the Cured to Get Sampled has become "A Canine Cone of Shame that Makes Us All Feel Same." A very specific type of Game. Can we collaborate, what would be the preconditions for acceptance?

The context was pretty... Illusory. Inscribed: “Before I was in a chain gang.” I knew what I meant. Why didn’t you? A fairly profound statement of hyperbole. “Because it wasn’t your story.”

It occurred to me, I'm writing stories... and there’s too much foot traffic around the curious not to see them as targeted. For some reason. For insight. Less interview ready, though. Verbs, that was what we needed. Activity that generated its own future. But it only counted if it wasn’t already measured.

A kind of measurement that came from, “Oh! Something was ignited. As compared to being deemed outside concern.” You know, the things on the tube screen displayed.

Adverts were popular, at the time.

“I, Jennifer Love-Hewitt am Jennifer Love-Hewitt. That's fairly obvious. What comes next might surprise you!”

The guide dictated otherwise, as long as the remote functioned. Function. A secret miracle.

- -## - - ##- -

“Please excuse the lack of order in the classroom.” There was a cause, shared and growing in the manner of movements initiated by missive. Hit or just plain.

"Ok class, recess!"
"Hey, look here, Mrs. Hazmat-Keenke-Kell, why we using this nigra science to access recess, we should be using our minds to roam about freely!"

"Well Mr. Wiley, why don't you ask yourself."

"They cain't reeeed my chicken scratch!"... *Dear God.*

Then:

Dearly Regarded Karmacodar Redcup Hound:

I was drawn into addressing yet another letter that wouldn't write itself! For lack of effort, probably. Was there any other kind?

The Capable Ride Into Town with Rescue Beneath Them, Unobserved

Origins of the origins were a source of contention. Stock stories having exhausted themselves, passively, in the purely descriptive. Passively!

It was either My life of bed rot or A bad day to stop short on candor. A day's name so anonymous, it ended in the suffix "day" in English. Complete with a shift to 'good becoming bad' as soon as it hit open atmosphere. Intoned, the phrase that would launch the thousands of words typically expended on evaluations.

*An intersex enemy *just like you* ended the Vikings. Organically. How will you react to its offspring?*

The conclusion was predictable.

"The tarbaby came from inside your vaginal house!" Then we made him determine her own paternity. But it was too confusing, the data, too plural a usage to be anything other than consensus on how to conspire to feed the goats hillside brush.

Fine. Confirmation test me, then. Confirmation bias test? Or blood test?

Ok, [sigh] CensusSays, first things first, I and iRobot. Are you available for the post-coital interview?
Sure, yeah.
Then sounds emerged that were amplified during the performance (of dinner theatre). A repeat, with references to reheated leftovers.

"Our life together begins now, Ms. Gerunded-Me. Show me 'dese in stock colors:"
"First, Paper-maichè Renewable Sex Machine?,"
Yep. Check!
"Tech-enabled Solicitous Bankruptcy?"
Check!
"Aborted Speech Cornsilk Patterns?"
Yep.
"Wholegasm (Denial) Exchange?'
Who is that??
"Simulcast Ded 'Em Tacocat?"
No effing way?!

Office of Maximum Expression asked us how they might be of service.
"Ok class, recess!"
The goal was to recall finally the time at the gym, the salubrious effect of hours moving muscle to enact flesh. Transmutation of time into a mountaintop adventure the Alpine air lent a crisp and lucid quality to. Even though...

"They cain't reeeed my chicken scratch!"

Or a face? The Circle R launched the Campaign for a New Offering at Circle Qué? Like liking same, in acceptance of the condition we are in being a product of memory-foam support and the correct topper.

From the caves of the Ali Baba region came a commandment: Mike says you're a bitch, you a bitch, use a bitch. Doubt was resolved on a history of pylon.

Now we don't need words. Castrate the disagreement.

To avoid literal diaster. "Solomon Saltmine yourself, Süleyman Pandemicide," was the reply.
"And you have the Putomija in position?"
But I thought...
#
Ok, Pace Frog. The bloom is off the rose; however, we are in need of a means through which meaning is used to construct the scafffolding surrounding the Race to Confront the Source of our Fears with olde style indifference to the appearance among us of a changeling. The kind originating in the first 600 years of Our Lady of Lordes, where our circle resolved to You. Are. Welcome. Out of necessity.

These people (those one, right there) get there on the Wings of Daffy. Scored by sacred, martial music translated to 'Murikan as the backdrop to a dead hampster kinetic-powered sleigh ride through some kind of non-overdetermined interior. Then comes the house they rode in on.

*I wonder if they are using Sum total, KPIs. The stuff that gives you protection from the FAX Hollowtech."
In thy name.
"You don't have to call me Dim Kip. Exercise your power of Free Will."

"Board of Erectors needs to see you in chambers. Proceed, please, directly to Chambers."
"There is no Erectmore Chamber.
"Not as long as you all are keeping time." Pause.
"I won't if they are using, KPIs."
Kip, my name is Kip.

- --

Our sense of the speed of their evolution changes. As we move through an atmosphere of pandemic insecurity, do you share a view on how to report that candidly?

The whole Dystopian Death Penalty Sentience Police was used to reinforce an object lesson about the reality of idealism, ideology and racism when people refuse to communicate through any method except virtue-signaling object lesson. We were to learn how virtue, when invoked in relationship to humans, meant 'an intangible quality whose positive or negative value depends on the relationship (collaborative, antagonistic or both) between subject (enacter) and object (described)'.

Length of construction masculine you female dominate dominate for union with length of conclusion."

Could it be? They only *look* like they are educated?

By way of explanation: There was too much difference between (Evil vs. Satan), the joy we express for *our* past and what expression we can support. Mostly around "It is disturbing, the signs of belief that the goal of keeping up appearances is eternal seriousness (Baby Factory batteries sold separately)."

That was having a negative effect on young people, the kids some say they had 'since before they were looking for [you]', and the kids that I saw there more regularly, two miles or more away.

"Get these pimps and bottoms up out of space! Learn 'em!"

Just like Jung > FreudFreudFreud. One type of collectivity is great, not as damaging long term. Shared history being more important than replication of vessels, the kind defined as a type of blank slate for access to control by Allstate, from the Giant Robot state.

"Teacher, Access says, control for x, let x = 3x," said FreudFreudFreud.
And then Snufalufagus asked, "Is he here, not here, or here? All three?"

Access was quoted:
In Ireland, long ago, it was believed ... that children were sometimes taken by fairies and replaced by a sickly fairy child called a 'Changeling'.

But how to cure a weak or sickly child?

The new child - the changeling - is characterized by unresponsiveness, resistance to physical affection, obstreperousness, inability to express emotion, and unexplained crying and physical changes such as rigidity and deformity. Some are unable to speak.

Myth had intruded, with its sense power which resided in awareness of the uncommon kind, married to a hopeful belief in chance.

Eminence Gris Grease Stains Complains for the First Time to Mrs. Yu

Your Child Is Not Your Own? The Origins Of the Changeling Myth [ed: In lore, Satan made a vagina out of his ballsweat, and he calls it "You, Pieces of Special."]

Medieval folklore and stories were full of strange people, unnatural beings and evil spirits. One such creature, a tale to haunt any family, was the changeling, historically known as an oaf or an auf.

The changeling appears again and again in folk tales throughout Europe. The changeling would appear in the bed of an infant, and superficially it resembled the child it replaced, but it was not human, and the original child had disappeared.

Three bean salad: what makes it wax and wayne, so magically?" Of course there was a myth about it! Called 'Once more, with feeling.'

SSRI Entrepreneur Chairmens of the Bored Directors has issued a timely memo designed to quell dissent!

Theirs is not a dimension, it's a mirror of a pattern called hate, if a pattern is what it can be, a renewal of disaster. Either that or a type of maturity made increasingly unconscious, like that feeling that starts somewhere innocuous, a place rarely seen by our own eyes. The produce of association.

And the disaster has an engine. Shields up, to deflect the lasting memories, those that change so little here they are predetermined by... diet.

"No! Not the Biodeterminism!"

All the isms. All the time. Single cut ham was broad enough to matter. And then we had not much left to wonder about but time.

Cat Skinner

and the Fruitless Fruit Eaters

Cat Skinner walks on his hands, even though he has boots, his friends complained in private. When they saw him, they asked, "What is down on the ground that you like so much, that is so appealing you walk with hands in boots and refuse to take your eyes away from it or use your feet?"
"I have no hands," said Cat Skinner, "I have only feet! What do you hate so much down there that my feet must become hands to you?"

They did not respond.

Cat Skinner thought long and hard, almost a full half day of one of his nine lives. They don't need hands, he thought, so they make my feet hands, so that they can take my boots!

The logic was impeccable.

He put his boots on his other feet and walked to a friend's house, and they greeted him with surprise.
"Oh, you've put your boots on your feet, finally! What a pleasant treat!"
"Anything to make you happy," said Cat Skinner, who was very quick on his feet, regardless of which ones he used, "you must have been very angry."

"It must be a relief for you to be looking, finally, at blue skies," they answered, showing some deft footwork of their own.
"Only because you make it so."

Cat Skinner was a perfect gentleman, of the kind that have no hands. "Do these pleasant skies comfort you?"

It was a picturesque day, not a cloud to be found that would not be soon whisked away by gentle afternoon sun.

"No, your escapades make me and others recall the fruit that lies in the ground, that does not grow. This sadness is what we try to avoid. But your visit has brightened this already bright day. I see much more pleasant weather in everyone's future, there is the spirit of compromise and renewal in the air, I might even take your hand one day and walk through the plains on our way to market, if you'll let me."
"That was all it took? My willingness to put your needs first?"

"Well, that was not what I wanted at the time, you looked so happy with your backwards ways that I worried things might never change, that I should only expect more of the same, whether you put on your boots correctly or not."
So, they never wanted my boots! Cat Skinner realized.
"What if I hadn't?" Cat Skinner asked. "What if I returned to my happiness and your concerns did not subside?"
"Well, our happiness is now intertwined, so let us both hope for blue skies from this day forward."

Cat Skinner walked around on his other feet for three days, but found it tiresome. The people he passed on the winding cow paths seemed focused, still, on the ground where their gaze always rested, but to Cat Skinner their happiness seemed beyond question, now that he knew the joys of blue skies for those who called their feet 'hands'. Upon his arrival at the Town Square, Cat Skinner saw people pointing at him and was praised as an exemplary citizen and proof of how our lives could change and improve. The sodden mood they suffered from in this land where the ground bore no fruit would surely soon pass.

Still, he realized that his back feet tired quickly in this mode of walking, and so he also began to see the ground as a tyrant, even when the skies were pleasant and a gentle breeze nudged at his back. Cat Skinner, always attuned to happiness, knew he could not change the ground, but he could help the townsfolk share in his happiness once again.

"They hate the ground for not bearing fruit, which I cannot change," he said, "but they also hate those who walk on their feet." It troubled him for two fortnights, until a burst of inspiration came to him.

Later, on the eve of his revelation, his used his feet to climb into their houses, and cut off all their hands.

"When they awaken, they will be so glad that they can now enjoy the simple pleasure of walking on feet that do not tire, and feel grateful to have been relieved of their belief in the importance of hands. Surely their hatred of the ground will dissipate, like the rain that falls from above to make the land feel its sadness."

The next day, the town bell tower rung ten times, an alarm call all knew signaled an emergency of the most dire kind. When Cat Skinner approached the square, boots on his front feet to show them the simple pleasure of reorienting oneself to true happiness, they all wailed and cried.

What's the matter?" Cat Skinner

asked, "Why are you no longer happy?"

You've returned to your old ways, and worse, in the cover of darkness someone snuck in our homes and cut off our hands! We can no longer harvest the orchards that bear the fruit that is our only source of sustenance!"

"If you put your boots on your hand stumps, then you can surely kick down the fruit using your legs, and in this way you can also be assured that you only pick fruit that is ready to be harvested!"

Overjoyed at having found a solution so quickly, they walked over to the orchard, although on their feet, according to their preferred custom, and kicked the trees until they were surrounded by so much fruit that they knew they would never be hungry again. They began to glimpse the cause of their misunderstanding, their fear the fruit would never grow to be theirs.

"Oh, thank you, Cat Skinner, you are truly an infinite source of happiness!" they all said in unison.

"It was not the ground you were angered by then," said Cat Skinner, "it was your unwillingness to use your feet."
"Yes, we accept now that you have only feet, and that our dislike was not for your orientation toward the ground, but the work required by us to wait for what is already there to become what we need."

"Oh, so you are glad now that I cut off your hands while you slept!"

The townspeople cried out in anguish, fury emerging from every pore of their body.

"It was you that almost cost us the fruit! It was you, you must have conspired with the ground, to be so happy with it, and your cruelty will certainly be punished!"
"But you were happy just a moment ago!"

The crowd moved toward him, brandishing farm tools and their look of hatred as weapons, and he realized only his boots stood between him and escape, so he shucked them quickly and sprinted away on his four feet.

I did not need these boots, I guess, he thought, it is wise to move on from them.

As he escaped, he looked back, to assess his safety, and it appeared as if his friends, arms waving wildly in the air, were attempting to say goodbye, but lacked the hands to do so.

What an odd goodbye, he thought, *but eventually, they will learn to say goodbye with their feet as I once greeted them with mine.*

About the Author

David J. Shepard melds fiction, non-fiction, journalism, poetry and content marketing techniques to depict the awareness of a thoroughly modern mind. Genre-agnosticism and hybrid forms reveal a literary world where texts are "content." In his work, popular culture is a point of departure for discussions of race, identity and difference.

He is the author of #**Blessed Be the Hellbound**, a work of hybrid fiction (Published by Ouroboros Press in November 2021), the short story collection **Outscape from Moontopia** (November 2022) and is the publisher and author of internetouroboros.com.